Unique Resistance Band Handbook:

Full Guide on Resistance Band a to z;Includes the Benefits of Resistance Band; Persons Eligible for It; Dos & Don'ts/Precautions & Storage & So Much More

By

Dr. Bradley L. Jackson

TABLE OF CONTENTS

CHAPTER ONE

INTRODUCTION

What are Resistance Bands?

Resistance bands are literally 'bands' that are flat or tubular in shape. Initially, their sole use was as a rehabilitation method for patients to get back to exercise post-injury. But now people are now combining them with their workout.

Resistance bands are rubbery in texture and they come in different sizes, colors, lengths, strengths. You can include them to your training to fire up your muscles.

CHAPTER TWO

Resistance Bands Colors and Meaning

So what do those various colors of resistance bands stands for.

The Yellow Bands

These are bands great for beginners. They are very stretchy and offer light resistance. It requires little effort to pull them against them. The bands are used to do some exercises which use joints such as shoulders and shins.

The Green Bands

The green resistance bands have more tension than the yellow resistance bands, green resistance bands are the next step up for beginner.

The Red Bands

These bands have higher tension level than the yellow and green bands. After your muscle strength have been buildup for some days and you are ready to improve more on your resistance challenging, you can go ahead and use your red resistance band. And they are used for muscle work such as chest, legs, and back.

The Blue Bands

They are very stiff and are heavy resistance. They require a bit of strength to pull compared to the red, green and yellow bands. They are for those that are very strong, or bigger muscle persons. It can also be best used when two people pull against a band.

The Black Bands

The heaviest resistance band to pull and stretch is the black resistance bands and it make workout quite challenging than the other colors of band. Black band are best used only when

you have a stronger muscle.

CHAPTER THREE

Types of Resistance Bands

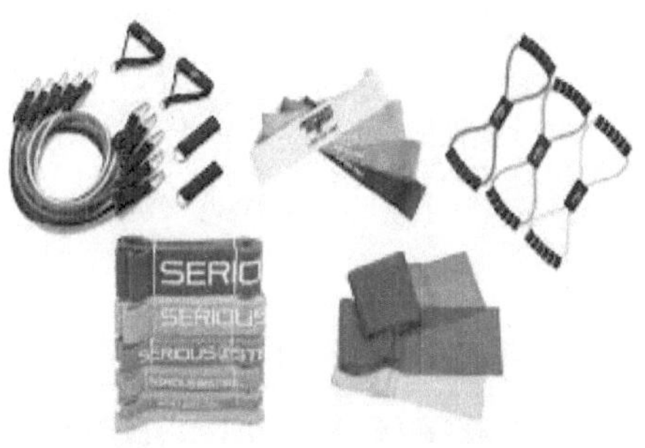

Therapy Flat Resistance Bands

These bands are often found in therapy settings, such as sports therapist or physical therapist offices. They are flat and wide, making themeasy to wrap around your hand and the length can be adjusted easily.

Loop Bands

These are bands that are used for strengthening the legs and buttocks. They are similar to therapy bands are smaller and form a closed loop. They can be seen in gyms and physical therapy offices.

Leg and Arm Tube Resistance Bands

These types of bands are more muscle-specific and limited in variety of exercises that can be performed. These bands come in several variations, such as figure-8 shapes with handles for upper body and leg band with ankle cuffs.

Resistance Bands with Handles

These tube bands are mainly used for working out and building muscles size and strength.When it comes to workouts, the handles on the resistance bands gives them the benefit of being able to be anchored just about anywhere, making it much easier to get a gym-like workout on the go.

Power and Mobility Bands

These are heavy duty bands they are most popular for cross-training and with power lifting. They also function for stretching and correcting mobility issues, adding variable resistance to weight training and pull-up assistance.

CHAPTER FOUR

Benefits of Resistance Bands

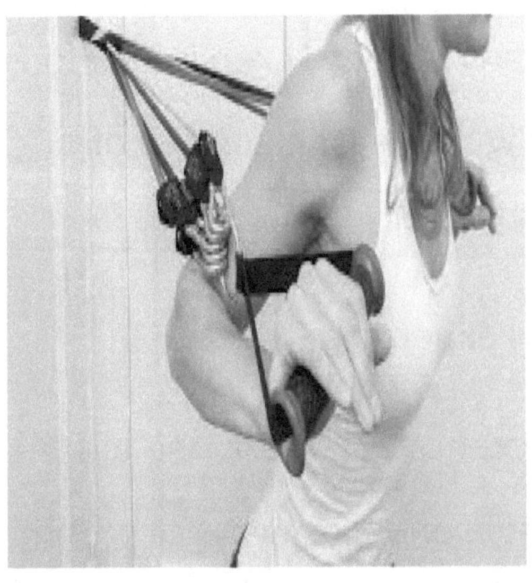

Easy to Learn

Resistance bands can be used to modify many familiar exercises. Even if you're a complete beginner and have never carried out any of these exercises before you will at least have idea of how it work.

Less expensive

Resistance bands are one of the most economical ways of getting fit.

The price of a resistance bands depend on the different types of resistance bands that you wish to buy.

Portable

They are very easy to carry around with you. Rather than purchasing equipment for exercise that will restricts you to working out at home, Try something else you can easily fit in your bag.

Resistance bands are very effective for getting in shape, their portable nature makes them to be carried around easily.

And resistance bands can be use anywhere.

Adaptable

The adaptability of resistance bands is one of their key strengths, and definitely commendations the fact that they can be taken anywhere.

Resistance bands are of different types and they come in various resistance strengths, they are similar to how dumbbells come in different weights!

The strength of resistance bands shouldn't be underestimated they can actually be pretty tough to master,it is tough when you start at a level that is too heavy for you.

The lighter the color the lighter the resistance... but ensure to read the packaging first!

Rehabilitation &Stretching

Resistance bands are commonly used for rehabilitative exercises. If you have suffered from wound in the past, chances are you have reaped the benefits of resistance bands which will lead you to recovery!

They are also used for stretching, since resistance bands are adaptable and come in light resistance levels.

Full-Body Workout

Anyone who has ever stared a new fitness routine, gaining a full-body workout is important.

With the use of resistance bands, it is possible to work

every part of your body. It is likely to be more effective with resistance tubes rather than flat bands, but that is not to say that you can't use them to start with!

CHAPTER FIVE

Who Should Use Resistance Bands?

After knowing the various types

of bands and the benefits of

resistance bands, it's probably

becoming clearer that anyone

can use resistance bands to reach their fitness goals. Here are some particular groups that should use them and why:

Anyone trying to lose Weight

Resistance training help you lose fat alone, rather than muscle. The healthiest way to lose weight is through exercise, since one need to burn more calories than consume to shad the pounds. Losing weight becomes easy when you combine a healthy diet cardio and strength training. You make sure bands such as full-body circuit, is added to your daily routine.

Anyone trying to Gain Muscle

If you are looking for how you can have more strength and gain muscle size. You can make use of resistance bands in place of dumbbells and machines to provide a new and challenging stimulus to the growth of your muscle.

Adults

For older adults around or over the age of 60, they standard weights at the gym can be challenging and harsh on their body. The use of resistance bands is one of the safest methods to increase bone strength and help prevent osteoporosis.

Athletes

Resistance helps prepare athletes it improves strength and it also prevents injuries. Is an important functional training

component for improving
athletic power as well as
improving flexibility and posture.
There is nothing better out there
to make you faster and stronger
than resistant bands. You can
easily carry them with you and
get a good work out no matter
where you are.

Pregnant Women

Exercise is very important during
pregnancy for improving sleep,
energy, mood and preparing for
childbearing. Resistance bands

are good for light muscle-toning.

You make use of one light and

medium band to hit all your

major muscles without stress.

SCHAPTER SIX

Simple Precautions to Make Band Workouts Safe

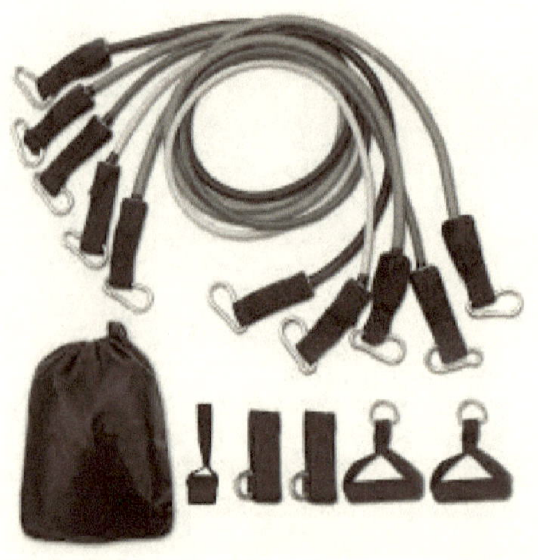

Tips to make sure your band

workout doesn't end with a trip

to the emergency room.

Inspect Resistance band daily

Make sure you use few seconds to inspect a band. Look for cracks in the white parts in colored bands and look if there is sign of weakness in the handle, the zone where wondercheck says bands are most likely to break.

Don't assume that bands at your gym are checked regularly. Check the band every time, and inform the gym officials about any damaged band.

Don't rely on your Instructor

Don't assume that band exercises your fitness instructor tells you to do are suitable. Ensure you learn the proper way to use your band, and if you are told to do something that isn't safe, don't do it. Politely let your instructor know isn't safe for you.

Put on good Shoes

Nonabrasive sole shoe should be used, when doing workouts that requires stepping on the band,

wondercheck said. This will
prevent the band from
damaging. Also, never use
resistance band with a bare feet.

Don't overstretch your band

Everything has an elastic limit.
Wondercheck recommend that a
band should not be extended
more than twice its resting
length.

Be aware

Don't use bands in hot places or
in direct sunlight, it will weaken

the bands. Avoid using your bands near pools. The chlorine will damage your bands.

Braided bands

Braided band offers an extra level of safety because if one braid of the resistance band snaps it simply unravels.

Remove Jewelry

Your jewelry can rub your bands and cause damage to it.

Never Release a band Under Tension

Your band builds up a lot of elastic energy as it stretches out. Don't let go of a stretched band as it can be dangerous to you or anyone around you.

Use bands on SmoothSurfaces

Resistance bands should not be used on rough uneven surfaces.

CHAPTER SEVEN

Bands Storage and Care

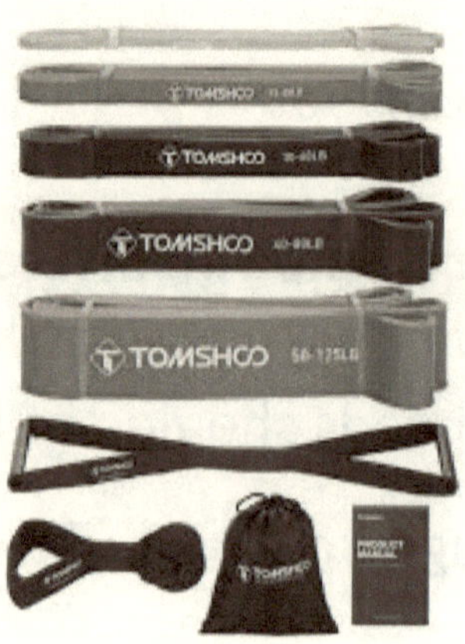

Clean your bands, by wiping them with a damp cloth.

Don't expose the bands to rough
or abrasive surfaces.

If your band becomes sticky,
clean with water, then flat dust
the band with talcum powder,
corn starch, or baby powder.

Your loop bands should be
stored away from direct sunlight
or extreme temperature (too
cold or too hot).

CHAPTER EIGHT

Quiz for You

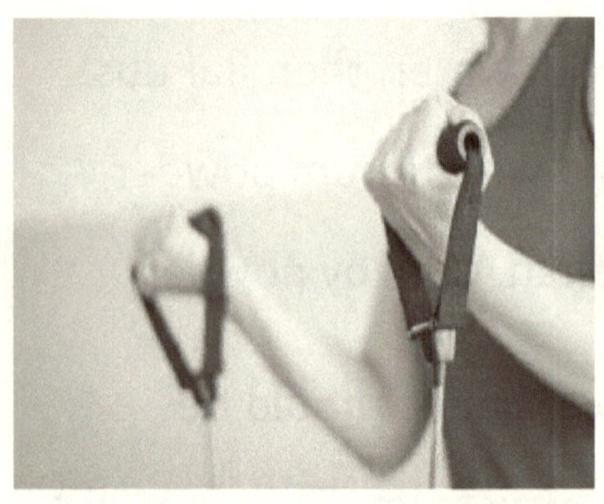

Resistance bands improve

strength & athletic performance.

TRUE/FALSE

It is advisable to use bands in

swimming pools TRUE/FALSE

Resistance bands are not without risk. TRUE/FALSE

Bands can be used to modify many familiar exercises. TRUE/FALSE

Tying off a band creates areas of friction on the bands that weaken it. TRUE/FALSE

Answers to Quiz

TRUE

FALSE

TRUE

TRUE

TRUE

CHAPTER NINE

Take away

Resistance band work out plan strengthens the whole body and triggers your core. Not only do the bands work, but you can make use of them anywhere. If you are the type that travels a lot, these bands will be great for your overall body balance, muscle strength and posture.

THE END